# RABBITS

# *What others are saying about this book*

*Rabbits: Gentle Hearts, Valiant Spirits* will enchant all animal lovers. This collection of true stories—of rabbits' innocence and tenacity, courage and high spirits—offers readers a glimpse of the nature and needs of these gentle beings. As the adoptive parent of a rescued bunny, this poignant book touched my heart and spoke to my soul.

—KISKA ICARD, director of program management for the San Francisco
Society for the Prevention of Cruelty to Animals

∿

One of the first steps towards developing care and compassion for animals is providing people with a better understanding of their behavior and their needs. Marie Mead's *Rabbits: Gentle Hearts, Valiant Spirits* takes this step through a series of heartwarming stories about individual rabbits who survive deplorable situations and the human companions who commit to helping them. Each page brings us closer to understanding the world of domesticated rabbits and increases our desire to ensure their well-being, now and in the future.

—JEANNE MCCARTY, vice-president and director of
Roots & Shoots for the Jane Goodall Institute

∿

One doesn't have to share a home with a rabbit to enjoy this absolutely captivating collection of stories about the joys and tribulations of life with bunny. But I warn you: this book may make the idea of a rabbit companion rather tempting! *Rabbits: Gentle Hearts, Valiant Spirits* is above all about love, respect, compassion, and acceptance. It persuasively reinforces the depth of the animal-human bond while at the same time gently reminding us that, as guardians, we must be forever vigilant because caring for a pet is a lifelong commitment.

—SUSAN TAYLOR, executive director of Actors and Others for Animals

∿

These heartwarming stories about rescued rabbits and the people whose lives they touched are sure to provide, as Cleveland Amory was fond of saying, "hope for the hopless." Rabbits are sometimes described as the animals God has forgotten, but Marie Mead remembers them with such warmth and passion that this book will teach us something about the merciful treatment we owe to rabbits and, indeed, to all creatures.

—MICHAEL MARKARIAN, executive vice president of The Humane Society
of the United States and president of The Fund for Animals

As a busy exotic animal practice, our staff has witnessed both good and bad animal treatment—not unlike the accounts in *Rabbits: Gentle Hearts, Valiant Spirits*. I value this exceptional book both for the heartwarming stories and for the lessons it provides on how to create the best life possible with (and for) a house rabbit.

—ANGELA M. LENNOX, DVM Dipl ABVP-Avian, president of the
Association of Exotic Mammal Veterinarians

~

When I read the eloquent Foreword by Dr. Michael W. Fox, I wondered if the rest of this book could possibly measure up. It did. Beautifully written stories focus on the positive outcomes of animal rescue, celebrating individual lives saved. All participants in this book deserve congratulations—the people who were able to recognize and appreciate the intrinsic worthiness of their bunnies and the marvelous rabbits who brought out the best in their humans. *Rabbits: Gentle Hearts, Valiant Spirits* will strike a chord in everyone who cares about animals.

—MARINELL HARRIMAN, founder of the House Rabbit Society,
author of *House Rabbit Handbook* and editor-in-chief of *House Rabbit Journal*

~

The stories of Kali, Kumar, and the other bunnies touched me in a way that I had not expected—who would have thought that such tiny souls could be such powerful teachers. Kudos to Marie Mead for enlightening the public on the plight of rabbits through these enchanting and bittersweet stories.

—SUSANA M. DELLA MADDALENA, executive director of PetSmart Charities

~

Marie Mead has done for rabbits what Jane Goodall has done for chimpanzees and Jeffrey Masson for farm animals. Pairing heartwarming true stories with clear, accurate, and concise information about rabbits' physical and emotional needs, this book shines a spotlight on their unique personalities. In story after story, rabbits reveal to their human companions their complex, always individual, temperaments. Rebounding from an often dire beginning, each rabbit demonstrates resilience, determination, and a tremendous capacity for giving and receiving love. This book will forever change the way we look at these remarkable creatures.

—JOANNE LAUCK (HOBBS), author of *The Voice of the Infinite in the Small* and
founder and executive director of Catalyst for Youth, Inc. and Heart of Chaos

*Rabbits: Gentle Hearts, Valiant Spirits* is a most appropriate title for an engaging book that I couldn't put down! Each story is a learning experience, educating while tugging at our heartstrings. Marie Mead has captured the essence of these gentle and highly intelligent creatures, revealing their virtues as loving and wonderful companions. Animal lovers, teachers, and parents should surely read this book to understand the plight of one of the most misunderstood and overlooked of pets—the domestic rabbit.

—BARI MEARS, founder and president of the Phoenix Animal Care Coalition
and coauthor of *Love Stories of Pets and Their People*

~

*Rabbits: Gentle Hearts, Valiant Spirits* educates, inspires, and charms us. But most importantly, it is a call to action. This important book helps us appreciate the special qualities of rabbits and motivates us to take responsibility, ensuring they are given the respect and care they deserve.

—MARY LOU RANDOUR, PhD, director of education for the
Doris Day Animal Foundation and author of *Animal Grace*

~

Here is a book that will be loved by friends of animals everywhere. In this splendid work, Marie Mead reveals the full complexity of rabbits—from their individual idiosyncracies to their common needs. The heart and spirit of these gentle creatures have found a voice.

—TOM REGAN, author of *Empty Cages* and co-founder with wife, Nancy,
of the Culture and Animals Foundation

~

Author Marie Mead clearly knows rabbits—her stories capture every nuance of rabbit personality from tenacity to mischief. Yet *Rabbits: Gentle Hearts, Valiant Spirits* is also a testament to people and the miracles that occur through a love that transcends the artificial boundaries of species. This is a book for all people who share their life with an animal or who have known the healing power of love.

—LUCILE C. MOORE, author of *A House Rabbit Primer*

~

This book is a blessing for all rabbits and for all who love them. It offers a touching blend of heartwarming stories and practical guidance for proper care of our kindred spirits.

—ALLEN M. SCHOEN, DVM, MS, author of *Kindred Spirits*

Keeping a rabbit in a hutch—like keeping a dog tethered—is, unfortunately, too often a socially acceptable practice. *Rabbits: Gentle Hearts, Valiant Spirits* challenges the conditions in which many rabbits exist and presents both facts and true stories to encourage a more vital, interactive life with these intelligent animals. This book will change the way rabbits are viewed by many in our culture, moving us closer to a just, compassionate, and peaceful society.

—KENNETH SHAPIRO, PhD, editor of *Society and Animals* and
co-executive director of Animals and Society Institute

Anyone who has had the honor of communing with a rabbit—nose to nose, whisker to cheek—will applaud this book. Those unfamiliar with these dear little creatures will enjoy the heartwarming tales of adversity overcome and joy achieved. Educating the public is of paramount importance to the welfare of rabbits, and the author has captured the essence of this far-reaching task. Our rescued rabbits give all who were involved in the creation of this book a "two paws up"!

—DIANA ORR LEGGETT, founder and president of Rabbits' Rest Sanctuary and WildRescue, Inc.

Marie Mead's collection of inspiring stories is truly enriching. I found myself experiencing a vast range of emotions as I read tales of amazing acts of acceptance and compassion. The stories prove that rabbits can be valuable teachers of life lessons and that there is no greater gift than unconditional love. Readers of *Rabbits: Gentle Hearts, Valiant Spirits* will gain a new respect for the strength of one of nature's most fragile creatures.

—ERIKA SMITH ROYAL, founder and president of Brambley Hedge Rabbit Rescue

With great respect and appreciation I bow to author Marie Mead. Through her compassion, dedication, and clarity of intent, she brings to light the magical and very real 'Beingness' of rabbits as sentient, courageous, and highly intelligent citizens of this planet. *Rabbits: Gentle Hearts, Valiant Spirits* adds a powerful boost to the emerging ethos that honors all life. Please read this book and give it to everyone you know.

—RITA REYNOLDS, author of *Blessing the Bridge* and editor of the quarterly journal, *laJoie*

# RABBITS

## Gentle Hearts • Valiant Spirits

*Inspirational Stories of Rescue, Triumph, and Joy*

Marie Mead

with Nancy LaRoche

Foreword by Dr. Michael W. Fox

**NOVA***maris* PRESS

For information write: Nova Maris Press, 977 Seminole Trail, #356, Charlottesville, VA 22901-2824.
www.novamarispress.com

Marie Grosshuesch holds the copyright to all content in this book except for the writings listed below:
Foreword © 2007 Dr. Michael W. Fox
"Drowned Rats" and "Frankie's Foible" © 2007 Nancy J. LaRoche
"Rabbit Teeth: The Importance of Proper Care" © 2007
    Dr. Angela M. Lennox
"Emily" © 2007 Susan Chernak McElroy
"Finding Quality Veterinary Care for Your Rabbit" © 2007
    Lucile C. Moore
"Born to Be *ME*!" © 2007 Bernie S. Siegel, MD
"The Rabbit Round-Up" is based on an original story by Caroline Gilbert that appeared in The Fund for Animals "Rabbit Sanctuary Newsletter." It was rewritten with her permission. Versions of two written pieces first appeared in issues of Joyce Leake's online-magazine, "Living with Animals: Stories of People and Animals"—"Love Your Rabbit: The Basics of Rabbit Care" (June 2002) and "Lobo and Blueberry" (October 2002).

The photos and illustrations depict the actual rabbits in the stories, with the exception of the New Zealand white in "The Rabbit Round-Up" and the photos used in "The Great Rabbit Rescue." The latter photos are from the second of the great rabbit rescues in which Best Friends Animal Society has been involved.

"Jingle Bells," J. Pierpont, 1857.
"We Wish You a Merry Christmas," composer unknown, traditional.
"If wishes were horses," traditional proverb and rhyme.

Mead, Marie.
    Rabbits : gentle hearts, valiant spirits :
inspirational stories of rescue, triumph, and joy /
Marie Mead ; with Nancy LaRoche ; foreword by Michael W.
Fox.
    p. cm.
    Includes bibliographical references and index.
    LCCN 2006932196
    ISBN-13: 978-0-9786226-0-2
    ISBN-10: 0-9786226-0-X

    1. Rabbits.  2. Human-animal relationships.
3. Animal welfare.    I. LaRoche, Nancy, 1941-  II. Title.

SF453.M378 2007            636.932'2
                           QBI06-600326

Design by Rudy J. Ramos
Cover photographs by Velly Oliver
Printed in China

# Dedication

This book is a tribute to Kali and her dearest rabbit friend, Kumar.
The two are treasured and inspiring beings who have brightened my life
in immeasurable ways.

Many other rabbits have played an important role, among them: two Angora rabbits, Muffin
and Milly; a lonely Holland lop named Kirby; steadfast partners, Prancer and Rosie;
a courageous little rabbit named Trooper; and intrepid bunnies Siobhan and Oscar-Schneidig.

Bill Reed Photography

# CONTENTS